A CHOCOLATE
Dream

A
CHOCOLATE
Dream

❖

*Delicious cakes, gâteaux, tortes and
desserts for every occasion*

BY

ROSEMARY WADEY

PARRAGON

First published in Great Britain in 1997 by
Parragon
Unit 13–17
Avonbridge Trading Estate
Atlantic Road
Avonmouth
Bristol BS11 9QD

A catalogue record for this book is available from the British Library.

ISBN: 0-7525-2228-0

Printed and bound in Italy

Edited, designed and produced by Haldane Mason, London

Acknowledgements
Art Director: Ron Samuels
Editor: Diana Vowles
Home Economists: Sue Ashworth, Carole Handslip, Cara Hobday, Rosemary Wadey, Pamela Westland
Design: Zoë Mellors
Photography: Joff Lee
Additional photography: Iain Bagwell, Amanda Heywood

Material contained in this book has previously appeared in
Classic Cakes, Cooking for One & Two and *Picnics* by Rosemary Wadey, *Cooking on a Budget* by Sue Ashworth, *Death by Chocolate* by Judy Bugg, *Farmhouse Teas* by Janice Murfitt, *Pancakes & Waffles* and *Puddings & Desserts* by Cara Hobday, *Quick & Easy Meals* by Carole Handslip and *Recipes with Yogurt* by Pamela Westland.

Note
Cup measurements in this book are for American cups.
Tablespoons are assumed to be 15 ml. Unless otherwise stated, milk is assumed to be
full-fat, eggs are standard size 3 and pepper is freshly ground black pepper.

CONTENTS

INTRODUCTION

Chocolate is a mouth-watering temptation adored by everone. But where exactly does it come from?

Chocolate is produced from the beans of the cacao tree, which originated in South America. These trees are also widely grown in tropical humid climates such as Africa, the West Indies, tropical parts of America and the Far East.

The cacao beans grow in large pods which range in colour from purple to yellow according to variety. They are harvested when ripe, then both the beans and the pulp from the pods are allowed to ferment in the sun. This lets the beans gradually develop a chocolate flavour while the pulp around them evaporates as they dry. The outer skin is removed and they are left in the sun for a further period or are roasted. Finally they are shelled to leave just the kernels for making into cocoa and chocolate.

It takes several processes to turn dried cacao beans into chocolate. They have to be ground and crushed between giant rollers first and then they go through other stages before a thick chocolatey mixture or paste called 'cocoa solids' is produced. Some of the fat or 'cocoa butter' is pressed out and the remaining dry cake is reduced to a fine powder which is then thoroughly sieved and blended to produce the familiar cocoa powder used in drinks and cooking. The cocoa solids which have been pressed are blended with cocoa butter and further refined to turn them into the chocolate we so love.

Chocolate has gained a reputation for many things – mainly as one of the most addictive foods available, creating numerous 'chocoholics' who crave this irresistibly sweet, calorie-laden indulgence in one or more of its many forms. It is also reputed to be possessed of aphrodisiac qualities and is definitely a quick energy supplier, probably because of its caffeine content. However, for an unfortunate small group of people, chocolate is the cause of migraines – a tempting delight that is sometimes considered worth the cost of a bad headache! It is mainly used for sweet rather than savoury dishes, but there

delicious Mexican dish that combines turkey, chillies and chocolate and many meat, game or poultry casseroles can be enhanced and enriched by adding a couple of squares of dark or bitter chocolate.

Chocolate is useful nutritionally as a concentrated form of energy and is valuable as a compact food for expeditions and for all kinds of travelling. The nutritional value of chocolate per 30 g/1 oz portion is approx 150 calories and 7.5–8.5 g fat in plain, milk and white chocolate. Continental chocolates are a little higher.

DRINKS FROM THE CACAO TREE

Cocoa powder

This is the powder left after the cocoa butter has been pressed from the roasted and ground beans. It is unsweetened for culinary uses and making the traditional 'cup of cocoa'. It is easy to use and has a strong, slightly bitter chocolate flavour, but it lacks the richness of block chocolate.

Powdered or drinking chocolate

This has powdered milk, sugar and flavourings blended into the basic cocoa powder to produce an almost instant drink. It was introduced in Britain in the mid 1700s, almost a century before blocks of eating chocolate were first available. It is also widely used in baking but adds extra sweetness as it is a sweetened product.

BLOCK CHOCOLATES

The quality of these chocolates varies according to the percentage of cocoa butter they contain – most types have approximately 30 per cent. The higher the percentage the richer and more intense the flavour, and the easier the chocolate becomes to melt and use. Flavour enhancers are also added. Most varieties of chocolate now have a luxury version which is richer, smoother and better flavoured. It is consequently higher priced but is a superior product for cooking. Most chocolate bars specify the cocoa solids content.

Dark chocolate

Contains 30–60 per cent cocoa solids with a pleasant, slightly sweet taste and dark colour. It is the most popular chocolate used for cooking. The higher the cocoa solids the richer and stronger the flavour, which is important as the other ingredients tend to dilute the chocolate flavour in a recipe. Many people like to eat plain chocolate in bar form – it is one of life's great indulgences!

Milk chocolate

This is more often eaten in bar form rather than used in cookery as it tastes creamy and sweet, due to the additions of sugar and condensed or powdered milk during production. It is a paler and richer brown colour than plain chocolate. It is good for adding a final decoration by drizzling or piping onto some other chocolate covering or decoration to give a contrast in

colour. As it melts quickly, care needs to be taken that it is the correct consistency for use in cooking.

White chocolate

This is creamy both in colour and texture and contains a lower percentage of cocoa butter than plain chocolate and no cocoa solids. The fat content is higher and it does not set as firmly as other chocolates. It needs care when melting, particularly in a microwave oven, for it tends to 'seize up' quickly unless handled carefully. Luxury white chocolate has a superior, less sweet and sickly flavour. It is very useful for decorations and for combining with dark chocolate to create attractive contrasts.

Couverture chocolate

This has a high cocoa butter content and is favoured by professional cooks. It retains a high gloss after melting and cooling and is very smooth tasting. It does, however, need 'tempering' before use to make it easier to work with. It comes in dark, milk and white varieties and is available from specialist suppliers.

Bitter or unsweetened chocolate

This has a high percentage of cocoa butter – on average 75 per cent – and no added sugar, as the name suggests. It is dark, with a strong, bitter, but rich flavour, excellent for use in confectionery, desserts and baking. It is available from larger supermarkets and specialist suppliers.

Chocolate-flavoured cake covering

Made from sugar, cocoa, vegetable oil and flavourings, this has a rather synthetic flavour. You can add a few squares to normal chocolate when melting, for its high fat content makes it easier to shape decorations, especially curls and caraque, but don't overdo it or the flavour will be impaired. It is available in dark, milk and white varieties.

Chocolate dots, buttons, strands, etc.

All of these are available in dark, milk and white varieties. They are used in baking and for decorations, especially in recipes for children.

STORING CHOCOLATE

The better quality the chocolate you buy the better the flavour, result and ease of use. Supermarkets have a tremendous turnover of chocolate so what you buy is always fresh, but do check the shelf life it has been given and keep to its 'use by' date for best results and flavour. Store in a cool dry place away from sunlight, well wrapped and away from strong odours which can be absorbed. Old chocolate will become dull with a whitish bloom, which is harmless but spoils the appearance. Most chocolates store well for up to a year.

Chocolate decorations such as leaves, curls, caraque and so on should be carefully packed in rigid airtight containers, interleaved between greaseproof paper or non-stick baking parchment. Storage life in a cool place is approximately four weeks for dark chocolate decorations and two weeks for white.

OLD FAVOURITES

There are so many delicious recipes to choose from that when it comes to picking old favourites someone's personal favourites are sure to be missing. However, those recipes featured in this chapter, if not already old favourites of yours, are sure to become so very quickly. Plain, milk, continental and white chocolate are all used extensively to flavour, decorate and enhance a wide variety of recipes.

A range of delicious chocolate desserts are to be found in this chapter which are ideal for both everyday eating and special occasions, including quick puddings and elegant desserts and, of course, traditional teatime favourites. Chocolate Roulade, Black Forest Gâteau and Sachertorte all come into the rich and elegant category, while slightly sticky and moist Chocolate Brownies can be eaten at any time at all. Everyone loves Chocolate Eclairs full of whipped cream for a deliciously wicked teatime treat – their close relation the profiterole which is topped with a rich chocolate sauce also makes a truly luscious dessert. For sheer chocolate hedonism, add a tablespoon of sifted cocoa powder to the choux pastry mixture to provide a double chocolate eclair!

RICH CHOCOLATE
Cake

A deliciously rich chocolate cake is an essential stand-by for elevenses or afternoon tea. Everyone has their favourite recipes, but this luxurious version should please most tastes.

INGREDIENTS

Serves 8–10

2 tbsp cocoa powder
2 tbsp boiling water
175 g/6 oz/³/₄ cup unsalted butter
175 g/6 oz/³/₄ cup caster (superfine)
    sugar

3 eggs
175 g/6 oz/1¹/₂ cups self-raising flour
60 g/2 oz/¹/₂ cup ground almonds

ICING (FROSTING):
125 g/4 oz/4 squares dark chocolate
60 g/2 oz/¹/₄ cup unsalted butter

1 egg
175 g/6 oz/1¹/₃ cup icing
    (confectioners') sugar, sifted
60 g/2 oz/2 squares white chocolate

METHOD

1. Grease and line the base of 2 × 20 cm/8 inch sandwich cake tins (layer pans) with non-stick baking parchment.
2. Blend the cocoa powder and boiling water together until smooth.

3. Beat the butter and sugar together until light and fluffy. Add the eggs one at a time, beating after each addition. Add the cocoa mixture and blend together.
4. Sift the flour into the bowl, add the almonds and fold into the mixture until blended.
5. Divide the mixture equally between the cake tins (layer pans) and level the tops with a palette knife (spatula). Bake in a preheated oven at 160°C/325°F/Gas Mark 3 for 30–35 minutes or until the cakes spring back when lightly pressed in the centre. Loosen the edges with a palette knife (spatula) and turn the cakes out on to wire racks to cool.

6. Meanwhile, make the icing. Melt the dark chocolate and butter in a bowl set over a pan of gently simmering water, stirring occasionally. When it is melted remove from the heat and beat in the egg. Stir in the icing (confectioners') sugar and mix until smooth and glossy.

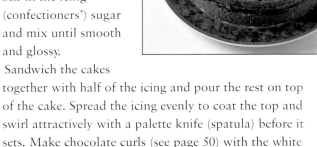
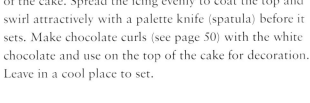

7. Sandwich the cakes together with half of the icing and pour the rest on top of the cake. Spread the icing evenly to coat the top and swirl attractively with a palette knife (spatula) before it sets. Make chocolate curls (see page 50) with the white chocolate and use on the top of the cake for decoration. Leave in a cool place to set.

CHOCOLATE
Roulade

A rich whisked mixture of eggs, sugar and dark chocolate to roll up with a filling of alcohol-flavoured fresh cream dredged with icing (confectioners') sugar.

INGREDIENTS

Makes 25 cm/10 inch roulade

175 g/6 oz/6 squares dark chocolate
5 eggs, separated
175 g/6 oz/³/₄ cup caster (superfine)
   sugar

few drops of vanilla flavouring
   (extract)
icing (confectioners') sugar
coarsely grated chocolate or
   chocolate curls to decorate
   (see page 50)

CREAM FILLING:
300 ml/¹/₂ pint/1¹/₄ cups double
   (heavy) cream
2–4 tbsp rum, brandy or liqueur

METHOD

1. Melt the chocolate in a bowl over a saucepan of gently simmering water, or in a microwave oven on Full Power for about 3 minutes. Stir until smooth.

2. Line a Swiss (jelly) roll tin (pan) of about 30 × 25 cm/ 12 × 10 inches with non-stick baking parchment. Whisk the egg yolks and sugar until very thick and creamy. Fold the melted chocolate through the egg yolk mixture with the vanilla.

3. Whisk the egg whites until very stiff and dry, and fold through the egg yolk mixture until blended. Spread out evenly in the prepared tin (pan), especially into the corners.

4. Bake in a preheated oven at 190°C/375°F/Gas Mark 5 for about 15–20 minutes, or until firm and crusty on top. Sprinkle a sheet of baking parchment very liberally with the sifted icing (confectioners') sugar. Invert the cake on to the paper and leave to cool slightly; then lay a damp tea towel (dish cloth) over the cake and leave until cold.

5. To make the filling, whip the cream until thick but not too stiff and fold in the alcohol. Put about 3–4 tablespoons of the filling into a piping bag (pastry bag) fitted with a large star nozzle (tip).

6. Peel the lining paper off the cake and spread the cake evenly with the cream.

7. Roll up the cake carefully with the help of the baking parchment and transfer to a serving plate. Pipe a line of the filling along the top of the cake and decorate with grated chocolate or chocolate curls.

BLACK FOREST
Gâteau

Layers of chocolate cake flavoured with Kirsch and sandwiched with cream and black cherries; add chocolate-coated sides and a cherry and cream decoration and you have pure luxury.

INGREDIENTS

Serves 8–10

3 eggs
140 g/4½ oz/½ cup plus 1 tbsp caster (superfine) sugar
90 g/3 oz/¾ cup plain (all-purpose) flour
20 g/¾ oz/3 tbsp cocoa powder

450 ml/¾ pint /2 cups double (heavy) cream
90 g/3 oz/3 squares dark chocolate
3–4 tbsp Kirsch, brandy or other liqueur
1 quantity Chocolate Butter Cream (see page 94)

FILLING:
425 g/14 oz can of stoned (pitted) black cherries, drained and juice reserved
2 tsp arrowroot

METHOD

1. Grease a deep 23 cm/9 inch cake tin (pan) and line with non-stick baking parchment. Whisk the eggs and sugar together until the mixture is very thick and pale in colour and the whisk leaves a heavy trail when lifted.

2. Sift the flour and cocoa powder together twice, then fold evenly and lightly through the mixture. Pour into the prepared tin (pan) and bake in a preheated oven at 190°C/375°F/ Gas Mark 5 for about 30 minutes, or until well risen and firm to the touch. Invert on a wire rack and cool.

3. To make the filling, reserve 8 cherries for decoration and halve the rest. Mix the cherries and 150 ml/¼ pint/ ⅔ cup of the juice with the arrowroot. Bring slowly to the boil, stirring continuously, and boil until clear and

thickened. Set aside to cool.

4. Whip the cream until thick enough to pipe and put 4 tablespoons into a piping bag (pastry bag) with a large star nozzle (tip). Pare the chocolate into curls (see page 50). Split the cake horizontally into 3 layers. Spread the first layer with some cream and half the cherry mixture.

5. Cover with the second cake layer, sprinkle with the liqueur, then spread with some of the butter cream and the remaining cherry mixture. Top with the final layer of cake. Cover the sides with the rest of the butter cream.

6. Spread the remaining whipped cream over the top of the gâteau and press the chocolate curls around the sides. Pipe 8 whirls of cream on the top. Add a cherry to each whirl. Chill for 2–3 hours.

SACHERTORTE

This rich chocolate gâteau was the invention of Franz Sacher, who owned a hotel in Vienna in the 1880s. There are now many recipes that copy his speciality, and this is one of the most delicious.

INGREDIENTS

Makes 23cm/9 inch cake

150 g/5 oz/5 squares dark chocolate
1 tbsp water
150 g/5 oz/³/₄ cup caster (superfine)
  sugar
150 g/5 oz/²/₃ cup butter
5 eggs, separated

few drops of vanilla flavouring (extract)
150 g/5 oz/1¹/₄ cups plain
  (all-purpose) flour, sifted
1 tsp baking powder
300 g/10 oz/generous ³/₄ cup apricot
  jam (preserves), sieved (strained)
1 quantity Chocolate Butter Cream
  (see page 94)

*CHOCOLATE ICING
  (FROSTING):*
175 g/6 oz/6 squares dark chocolate
175 ml/6 fl oz/³/₄ cup water
good knob of butter
125 g/4 oz/²/₃ cup caster (superfine)
  sugar

METHOD

1. Grease a 23 cm/9 inch springform tin (pan) and line with non-stick baking parchment. Dust with flour. Melt the chocolate with 1 tablespoon water in a bowl over a pan of simmering water.
2. Cream the sugar and butter together until light and fluffy. Beat in the egg yolks one at a time, then beat in the melted chocolate and vanilla. Fold the sifted flour and baking powder into the mixture. Whisk the egg whites until very stiff and beat a tablespoonful into the mixture, then fold in the rest evenly.
3. Spoon the mixture into the lined tin (pan), level the top and bake in a preheated oven at 150°C/300°F/Gas Mark 2 for about 1 hour, or until well risen and firm. Cool in the tin (pan) for 3 minutes, then invert on a wire rack.

4. When it is cold, split the cake in half and spread with half of the jam (preserves). Reassemble the cake and spread the remaining jam (preserves) all over the cake.

5. To make the icing (frosting), melt the chocolate with 2 tablespoons of the water, as in step 1. Stir in the butter until melted. Boil the remaining water with the sugar until syrupy. Pour over the chocolate and beat until smooth. Leave to cool, beating occasionally, until thick enough to stick to the cake. Pour over the cake and spread to cover the sides and top evenly.
6. Use a piping bag (pastry bag) and small star nozzle (tip) to pipe chocolate butter cream stars around the edge and base of the cake. Use a plain writing nozzle (tip) to write 'SACHER' across the top.

CHOCOLATE
Eclairs

*Everyone's favourites – these light choux fingers (shells) are filled with cream
and topped with chocolate or coffee icing (frosting).*

INGREDIENTS

Makes 12–14

CHOUX PASTE:
75 g/2¹/₂ oz/¹/₂ cup plus 2 tbsp plain
    (all-purpose) flour
pinch of salt
60 g/2 oz/¹/₄ cup butter or margarine

150 ml/¹/₄ pint/²/₃ cup water
2 eggs, beaten

FILLING:
300 ml/¹/₂ pint/1¹/₄ cups double
    (heavy) cream or 1 quantity of
Pastry Cream (see page 94)

TOPPING:
125 g/4 oz/4 squares dark chocolate
    or white chocolate

METHOD

1. Grease 2 baking sheets. Sift the flour and salt together.
   Put the butter or margarine together with the water into
   a saucepan and heat gently until the fat melts, then
   bring to the boil.

2. Add the flour all at once and beat vigorously until the
   paste is smooth and
   forms a ball that leaves
   the sides of the
   saucepan clean. Remove
   from the heat and
   spread the paste out
   over the base of the
   saucepan. Leave to cool
   for about 10 minutes.

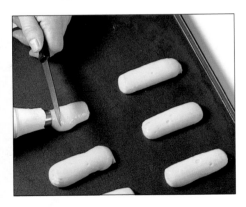

3. Beat in the eggs
   gradually until the
   mixture is smooth,
   glossy and of a piping consistency. It may not need all of
   the egg. A hand-held electric mixer is ideal for this.

4. Put the choux paste into a piping bag (pastry bag) fitted
   with a plain 2 cm/³/₄ inch nozzle (tip) and pipe in
   straight lines about 6 cm/2¹/₂ inches long, spaced well
   apart on the baking sheets. Cut the ends of the paste
   from the nozzle (tip).

5. Bake in a preheated oven at 220°C/425°F/Gas Mark 7
   for about 20–25 minutes, or until well risen, firm and a
   pale golden brown. Make a slit in the side of each éclair
   to let the steam
   escape, and return to
   the oven to dry out
   for a few minutes.
   Transfer to a wire
   rack to cool.

6. Whip the cream until
   stiff and use to fill
   each éclair, or use the
   pastry cream to fill
   the éclairs. Melt the
   chocolate in a bowl
   over simmering water, or in a microwave oven set on Full
   Power for 2 minutes. Remove from the heat and leave to
   cool until just beginning to thicken. Dip the top of each
   éclair into the chocolate, or spread with a palette knife
   (spatula). Leave to set.

PROFITEROLES

These cream and chocolate puffs are a favourite dessert for almost everyone,
and are unbelievably easy to make.

INGREDIENTS

Serves 8

150 ml/¹/₄ pint/²/₃ cup water
60 g/2 oz/¹/₄ cup butter
75 g/2¹/₂ oz/¹/₂ cup plus 2 tbsp plain
    (all-purpose) flour, sifted
pinch of salt
2 eggs, beaten

300 ml/¹/₂ pint/1¹/₄ cups whipping
    cream
sifted icing (confectioners') sugar, for
    dusting

RICH CHOCOLATE SAUCE:
250 g/8 oz/8 squares bitter
    (semi-sweet) chocolate

2 tbsp golden (light corn) syrup
2 tbsp coffee flavouring (extract)
300 ml/¹/₂ pint/1¹/₄ cups single
    (light) cream
2 tbsp dark rum

METHOD

1. Grease 2 or 3 baking sheets and sprinkle with a few drops of water. Put the measured water and butter into a saucepan over a low heat until the butter melts, then bring to the boil. Add the flour and salt together and beat until the mixture is smooth and leaves the sides of the pan clean. Remove the pan from the heat.

2. Beat the eggs into the pan a little at a time until thoroughly blended and the mixture is smooth and glossy (a hand-held electric mixer is best for this job).

3. Spoon the mixture into a large piping bag (pastry bag) fitted with a large plain vegetable nozzle (tip). Pipe small balls, about the size of a walnut, on to the baking sheets, leaving plenty of space between them to allow them to rise.

4. Bake in a preheated oven at 200°C/400°F/Gas Mark 6 for about 20 minutes or until risen and golden brown. Remove from the oven and make a small hole in each

puff to allow the steam to escape. Return to the oven for about 5 minutes to dry out slightly. Transfer to a wire rack and leave to cool.

5. Whip the cream until just stiff and spoon into a piping bag (pastry bag) fitted with a small plain vegetable nozzle (tip). Either insert the nozzle (tip) in the small hole made in the puffs for the steam to escape and pipe in the cream, or split the puffs in half and fill with cream. Pile the profiteroles in a pyramid shape on a serving dish and dust lightly with sifted icing (confectioners') sugar.

6. To make the chocolate sauce, place the chocolate, syrup, coffee and cream in a heavy-based saucepan and stir over a low heat until smooth and glossy. Stir in the rum, remove from the heat and leave to cool (the sauce will thicken as it cools). Pour the sauce over the profiterole pyramid and chill until required to serve.

AMERICAN
Brownies

*These are the moist and slightly chewy chocolate and nut American specialities
which are now popular everywhere.*

INGREDIENTS

Makes 20

125 g/4 oz/4 squares dark chocolate,
  broken into pieces
150 g/5 oz/²/₃ cup butter or margarine

350 g/12 oz/1¹/₂ cups caster
  (superfine) sugar
¹/₂ tsp vanilla flavouring (extract)
4 eggs, beaten
150 g/5 oz/1¹/₄ cups self-raising flour

90 g/3 oz/³/₄ cup pecans, walnuts,
  hazelnuts or almonds, chopped
60 g/2 oz/¹/₃ cup raisins
icing (confectioners') sugar for
  dredging

METHOD

1. Line a rectangular tin (pan), measuring about 28 × 18 × 4 cm/ 11 × 7 × 1¹/₂ inches, with non-stick baking parchment.

2. Put the chocolate and butter or margarine into a heatproof bowl and either place over a saucepan of gently simmering water and heat until melted, or melt in a microwave oven set on Full Power for about 2 minutes. Stir until quite smooth.

3. Remove from the heat and beat in the sugar and flavouring (extract) until smooth, followed by the eggs.

4. Sift the flour and fold through the mixture, followed by the chopped nuts and raisins.

5. Pour into the prepared tin (pan) and bake in a preheated oven at 180°C/350°F/Gas Mark 4 for about 45–50 minutes, or until well risen, firm to the touch, and just beginning to shrink away from the sides of the tin (pan). Leave to cool in the tin (pan).

6. Dredge heavily with sifted icing (confectioners') sugar and cut into 20 squares or fingers (bars). Store in an airtight container. The brownies will keep well for a week.

NOTE
*Brownies can be frozen successfully for up to 3 months,
but it is best to add the icing (confectioners') sugar after thawing.
If preferred, the Brownies may be topped with chocolate butter cream
(see page 94) sprinkled with grated dark or white chocolate;
or simply be swirled with melted dark or white chocolate.*

GRANNY BOB'S
Chocolate Pudding

A deliciously moist pudding, served piping hot to the table.
Softly whipped cream is a wonderful addition.

INGREDIENTS

Serves 4–6

60 g/2 oz/¹/₄ cup butter, softened
125 g/4 oz/¹/₂ cup caster (superfine)
  sugar
60 g/2 oz/2 squares dark chocolate

2 eggs, lightly beaten
125 g/4 oz/1 cup self-raising flour

SAUCE:
300 ml/¹/₂ pint/1¹/₄ cups milk
60 g/2 oz/¹/₄ cup butter

60 g/2 oz/2 squares dark chocolate,
  broken into pieces
3 tbsp granulated sugar
2 tbsp golden (light corn) syrup

METHOD

1. Grease a 1.1 litre/2 pint/4¹/₂ cup pudding basin. In a separate bowl, beat the butter and sugar together until pale.

2. Meanwhile, melt the chocolate in a bowl set over a pan of barely simmering water for about 10 minutes. Stir the chocolate into the butter mixture.

3. Beat in the eggs, one at a time, beating well after each addition.

4. Sift the flour into the bowl and fold in thoroughly.

5. Put all the sauce ingredients into a saucepan and heat through gently, without boiling, for about 10 minutes, until the chocolate has melted. Whisk well to combine.

6. Pour the sponge mixture into the greased pudding basin and pour the sauce over the top.

7. Bake in a preheated oven at 190°C/375°F/Gas Mark 5 for about 40 minutes. Serve piping hot from the bowl, or turned out on to a serving dish.

MELTING CHOCOLATE
Chocolate for decoration must be melted slowly in order to prevent it from
'seizing', which results in the chocolate being very granular and unworkable.
To avoid this, chocolate must not come into contact with droplets of water or
be heated to too high a temperature too quickly – treat chocolate with care.

WHITE & DARK
Chocolate Mousse

Although this looks stunning it is in fact very simple to make with the aid of a couple of large bowls and a good hand whisk.

INGREDIENTS

Serves 6–8

100 g/3¹/₂ oz/3¹/₂ squares dark
   chocolate
100 g/3¹/₂ oz/3¹/₂ squares good-quality
   white chocolate
4 egg yolks

2 tbsp brandy
1 sachet (envelope) or 1 tbsp
   powdered gelatine
50 ml/2 fl oz/¹/₄ cup hot water
300 ml/¹/₂ pint/1¹/₄ cups double
   (heavy) cream
4 egg whites

TO DECORATE:
100 g/3¹/₂ oz/3¹/₂ squares good-quality
   white or dark chocolate
1 tbsp lard (shortening)
cocoa powder

METHOD

1. Break the dark and white chocolate into pieces and put them into separate heatproof bowls. Set the bowls over saucepans of barely simmering water and melt the chocolate.

2. When melted, remove the bowls and beat 2 egg yolks into each, until smooth. Stir the brandy into the dark chocolate mixture. Set aside to cool, stirring the chocolate frequently.

3. Heat the gelatine and hot water in a heatproof bowl, set over a pan of barely simmering water, until it is clear, about 10 minutes. Stir half of the gelatine into each chocolate mixture until smooth.

4. Whip the cream until softly stiff, and whisk the egg whites until stiff.

5. Stir half of the cream into each chocolate mixture, then fold half of the egg whites into each mixture.

6. Pour or spoon both mousses at the same time into a 900 ml/ 1¹/₂ pint/3¹/₂ cup soufflé dish, one in each half of the dish, so that they meet in the middle but do not run into each other. Chill the mousses until ready to serve.

7. Break the chocolate for decorating into pieces and put into a heatproof bowl. Set over a pan of barely simmering water until melted, then stir in the lard (shortening) and pour into a small loaf tin (pan). Chill until set, then turn out.

8. To decorate, shave large curls of chocolate from the block with a vegetable peeler. Arrange attractively on the mousse, and dust with cocoa powder.

FLORENTINE
Twists

These famous and delicious Florentine biscuits (cookies) are twisted into curls or cones as they are removed from the baking sheets and then the ends are dipped in chocolate.

INGREDIENTS

Makes about 20

90 g/3 oz/$^1/_3$ cup butter
125 g/4 oz/$^1/_2$ cup caster (superfine)
   sugar
30 g/1 oz/3 tbsp raisins, chopped

60 g/2 oz/$^1/_2$ cup blanched or flaked
   (slivered) almonds, chopped
   roughly
45 g/1$^1/_2$ oz/scant $^1/_4$ cup glacé
   (candied) cherries, chopped
45 g/1$^1/_2$ oz/$^1/_4$ cup chopped mixed peel

30 g/1 oz/3 tbsp dried apricots,
   chopped finely
finely grated rind of $^1/_2$ lemon or
   $^1/_2$ small orange
about 125 g/4 oz/4 squares dark or
   white chocolate

METHOD

1. Line 2–3 baking sheets with non-stick baking parchment. Grease 4–6 cream horn tins (moulds) or a fairly thin rolling pin, or wooden spoon handles.
2. Melt the butter and sugar together gently in a saucepan and then bring to the boil for 1 minute. Remove the pan from the heat and stir in all the remaining ingredients, except the chocolate. Leave to cool.

3. Put 3–4 heaped teaspoonfuls of the mixture on to each baking sheet, spacing them well apart. Flatten slightly.
4. Bake in a preheated oven at 180°C/350°F/Gas Mark 4 for 10–12 minutes, or until golden brown. Leave to cool until they begin to firm up. As they cool, press the edges back to form a neat shape. Remove each one carefully with a palette knife (spatula)

and wrap quickly around a cream horn tin (mould), or lay over the rolling pin or spoon handles. If they become too firm to bend, return to the oven briefly to soften them again.

5. Leave until cold and crisp and then slip carefully off the horn tins (moulds) or remove from the rolling pin or spoons.
6. Melt the chocolate in a heatproof bowl over a saucepan of hot water, or in a microwave oven set on Full Power for about 2 minutes, and stir until smooth. Either dip the end of each Florentine twist into the chocolate or, using a pastry brush, paint chocolate over the bottom half of the twist. As the chocolate sets, decorate with wavy lines made with a fork. Leave to set.

CHOCOHOLIC INDULGENCES

What is the definition of a chocoholic? The answer is simple – anyone who is a devoted chocolate lover and can devour it at any time of the day or night falls into this category. The cause of this passion is unknown, but probably stems from being given just a small piece of chocolate for a treat as a small child!

Pure pleasure is gained from devouring rich and very chocolatey creations and the real chocoholic has no apparent guilty conscience! The rich Devil's Food Cake and Chocolate Fudge Cake will certainly satisfy the most avid chocoholic, as will the deliciously moist Rum Truffles flavoured with ginger and coated in chocolate, and the Mocha Boxes with their thick chocolate outer casing. The Chocolate Bread Pudding enhances everyone's favourite warming winter pudding with a delicious chocolate flavouring, while the chocolate icing (frosting) and decorations can be added to any dessert to satisfy the true chocoholics cravings!

CHOCOLATE
Marquis

*A fabulously rich dessert that requires only a smidgen on each plate.
If you feel it needs something else, serve with crème fraîche or fresh fruit,
and make chocolate leaves to decorate.*

INGREDIENTS

Serves 6–8

500 g/1 lb dark chocolate
125 g/4 oz/¹/₂ cup unsalted butter

30 g/1 oz/2 tbsp caster (superfine)
    sugar
4 whole eggs
1 tbsp plain (all-purpose) flour

METHOD

1. Line a 20 cm/8 inch springform tin (pan) with non-stick baking parchment.

2. Melt the chocolate, half of the butter and half of the sugar together in a heatproof bowl set over a saucepan of barely simmering water.

3. Beat the eggs and remaining sugar together until pale. Fold in the flour carefully.

4. Pour the chocolate mixture on to the batter and stir in gently with a wooden spoon.

5. Fold together with a whisk, lightly, but until well combined.

6. Pour the mixture into the lined tin (pan) and bake in a preheated oven at 230°C/450°F/Gas Mark 8 for 12 minutes only. It should still be slightly wobbly in the centre.

7. Run a knife between the edge of the dessert and the tin (pan), and then release the tin (pan). Tighten the tin (pan) again, and leave the marquis in the tin (pan) to cool. Freeze for at least 2 hours or until required.

8. Remove from the freezer at least an hour before serving to allow the dessert to come to room temperature. Cut into small slices to serve.

CHOCOLATE LEAVES

*Chocolate leaves make a very attractive decoration on the plate, and are simple to make.
Select some prettily shaped leaves from the garden and rinse them well. Drain and pat them dry with paper
towels – they must be bone-dry. Melt some chocolate in the top of a double boiler or in a heatproof bowl set over a
saucepan of simmering water. Use a grease-free paintbrush or pastry brush to brush the underside of the leaves
with the melted chocolate. Make sure that the chocolate is thick where the leaf meets the stalk.
Paint on 2 or 3 layers, allowing the chocolate to dry briefly between each layer.
Spread them out on a tray to dry, and pop them into the freezer for 10 minutes to harden.
When you are ready to use the chocolate leaves, simply peel the leaf from the chocolate.*

DARK RUM
Truffles

These tempting little treats are just the thing to serve after dinner. The rum or coffee-flavoured liqueur and date filling adds a rich but elegant touch.

INGREDIENTS

Makes 16

125g/4 oz/²/₃ cup stoned (pitted) dates, roughly chopped

175 g/6 oz stale ginger cake
60 g/2 oz/¹/₂ cup toasted chopped hazelnuts

3 tbsp coffee-flavoured liqueur or dark rum
250 g/8 oz/8 squares dark chocolate
sifted cocoa powder (optional)

METHOD

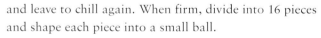

1. Put the dates into a saucepan and pour over enough water to cover. Cover the pan and simmer gently for 15 minutes. Remove the lid and cook until all the liquid has evaporated.

2. Put the dates, cake, nuts and liqueur or rum into a bowl and mix thoroughly, or place in a food processor and work until smooth. Leave to chill until firm enough to handle. If it is still too soft, add a few more cake crumbs and leave to chill again. When firm, divide into 16 pieces and shape each piece into a small ball.

3. Melt the chocolate in a heatproof bowl placed over a saucepan of simmering water, making sure the bowl does not touch the bottom of the pan and that the water does not splash into the bowl. Alternatively, heat the chocolate in a microwave oven set on Full Power for about 3¹/₂ minutes or until melted.

4. Carefully dip the truffles in the melted chocolate and turn to coat. Leave the truffles to set on sheets of non-stick baking parchment.

5. When the chocolate has set, transfer the truffles to petit fours paper cases and store in an airtight container in a cool place for up to 2 weeks. Sprinkle each truffle very lightly with sifted cocoa powder, if using.

TIPS
If ginger isn't your favourite flavour, use golden (light) corn syrup cake for this recipe. Alternatively, substitute chocolate cake instead for a truly chocoholic indulgence.

CHOCOLATE PEPPERMINT
Fondants

These are easy for either children or adults to prepare, and they make ideal treats and gifts. You can jazz them up by adding decorations, such as whole nuts or crystallized violets, while the chocolate is still wet.

INGREDIENTS

5 tsp glycerine
$^{1}/_{2}$ egg white, beaten
250 g/8 oz/1$^{1}/_{3}$ cups icing
    (confectioners') sugar, sifted

a few drops of green food colouring
a few drops of peppermint flavouring
    (extract)
250 g/8 oz/8 squares dark chocolate

30 g/1 oz/1 square white or milk
    chocolate, for decorating

METHOD

1. Stir the glycerine and egg white into the sifted icing (confectioners') sugar until well mixed. Add, drop by drop (or from the tip of a skewer if using paste colouring), enough food colouring and peppermint flavouring (extract) to colour and flavour to your taste.

2. Lightly dust a work surface with sifted icing (confectioners') sugar, and knead the peppermint mixture until smooth. Wrap in cling film (plastic wrap) and leave to rest overnight.

3. Knead again and roll out to a thickness of 5 mm/$^{1}/_{4}$ inch. Using a 2.5 cm/1 inch plain cutter, cut out rounds and lay on sheets of non-stick baking parchment.

4. Melt the chocolate in a heatproof bowl placed over a saucepan of simmering water. Make sure the bowl does not touch the bottom of the pan and that water does not splash into the bowl. Alternatively, heat in a microwave

set on Full Power for about 3$^{1}/_{2}$ minutes or until melted.

5. Carefully dip each peppermint fondant quickly in the melted chocolate. Shake off the excess, then carefully transfer to the baking parchment, or stand on a wire cooling rack so that the excess chocolate can drip through. (Some fondants may be only half dipped in chocolate, if liked).

6. If liked a whole nut, a crystallized violet, a piece of glacé (candied) cherry and so on can be placed on top of the fondants while the chocolate is still wet; or leave until set and decorate with a

swirl of melted white or milk chocolate placed in a paper icing bag (pastry bag) with just the tip cut off.

MOCHA
Boxes

*A delicious coffee and chocolate-flavoured cake smothered with butter cream
is enclosed within tempting chocolate boxes.*

INGREDIENTS

Makes 16

350 g/12 oz/12 squares dark
    chocolate-flavoured cake-covering
16 chocolate matchsticks, to decorate

CAKE MIXTURE:
175 g/6 oz/³/₄ cup butter or margarine

175 g/6 oz/1 cup light soft brown
    sugar
175 g/6 oz/1¹/₂ cups self-raising flour
90 g/3 oz/²/₃ cup plain (all-purpose)
    flour
3 eggs
1 tbsp sifted cocoa powder
1 tbsp coffee flavouring (extract)

MOCHA BUTTER CREAM:
125 g/4 oz/¹/₂ cup butter or margarine
250 g/8 oz/1¹/₃ cups icing
    (confectioners') sugar, sifted
1 tbsp sifted cocoa powder
2–3 tsp coffee flavouring (extract)

METHOD

1. Line a 20 cm/8 inch deep square cake tin (pan) with
non-stick baking parchment. Make up the cake as for
the Madeira (Pound) Cake on page 95, using the cake
mixture ingredients above and substituting cocoa
powder and coffee flavouring (extract) for the lemon and
citron peel. Put the mixture into the tin (pan), level the
top and bake in a preheated oven at 160°C/325°F/Gas
Mark 3 for 1–1¹/₄ hours, until well risen and firm and a
skewer inserted in the
centre comes out clean.
Invert on to a wire rack
and leave to cool.

2. Trim the cake and
cut into 16 squares
(5 cm/2 inches each).

3. Melt the chocolate
in a bowl over a pan of
simmering water or in
a microwave oven set

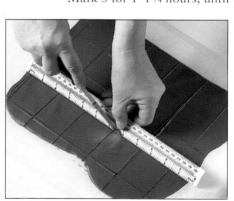

on Full Power for 4 minutes.
Spread the chocolate in a
40 cm/16 inch square on a
sheet of parchment. Pick up
one corner of the paper and
shake lightly to level the
chocolate. Leave until set.

4. Using a sharp knife and a
ruler, cut the chocolate into
64 × 5 cm/2 inch squares.
Chill until completely set.

5. To make the butter cream,
blend the butter, sugar,
cocoa powder and coffee flavouring (extract). Spread
over the sides and top of each cake square; put the rest
in a piping bag (pastry bag) with a star nozzle (tip).

6. Press a square of chocolate to each side of the cake
squares, then pipe a large whirl of butter cream on top
of each box. Decorate with 2 or 3 chocolate matchsticks.

CHOCOLATE FUDGE
Cake

Thin slices of this very rich and irresistible cake, served with a little pouring cream, make an unforgettable end to almost any meal. Serve without the cream for a wonderful teatime treat.

INGREDIENTS

Serves 8–10

90 g/3 oz/3 squares dark chocolate
175 g/6 oz/³⁄₄ cup butter
300 g/10 oz/1²⁄₃ cup light soft brown
    sugar
2 eggs, beaten

150 ml/¹⁄₄ pint/²⁄₃ cup boiling water
300 g/10 oz/2¹⁄₂ cups plain
    (all-purpose) flour, sifted
1¹⁄₂ tsp bicarbonate of soda
    (baking soda)
1 level tsp baking powder
150 ml/¹⁄₄ pint/²⁄₃ cup soured cream

1 tsp vanilla flavouring (extract)
2 quantities Chocolate Fudge Icing
    (Frosting) (see page 48)
icing (confectioners') sugar, for
    decorating

METHOD

1. Grease and line the bases of 3 × 20 cm/8 inch loose-based sandwich cake tins (layer pans) with non-stick baking parchment. Melt the chocolate in a heatproof bowl set over a saucepan of gently simmering water, making sure the bowl does not touch the bottom of the pan or water splash into the chocolate. Alternatively, heat in a microwave set on Full Power for about 1¹⁄₂ minutes, or until melted.

2. Cream the butter and brown sugar together until light and fluffy, and pale in colour. Beat in the eggs one at a time.

3. Beat the melted chocolate and boiling water together, leave to cool slightly then mix into the creamed mixture.

4. Sift the flour, bicarbonate of soda (baking soda) and baking powder together and fold into the chocolate mixture, alternating with the soured cream and vanilla flavouring (extract).

5. Divide the mixture between the cake tins (layer pans) and bake in a preheated oven at 190°C/375°F/Gas Mark 5 for about 25 minutes or until firm to the touch. Leave to cool in the tins (pans) then turn out on to wire racks.

6. Sandwich the cakes together with a little icing (frosting) between the layers and use the remainder to coat the top and sides of the cake. Mark an attractive design into the icing (frosting) as it cools using a palette knife (spatula) and leave to set. A little sifted icing (confectioners') sugar may be dredged over the cake, if liked.

DEVIL'S FOOD
Cake

This rich dark chocolate layer cake with a white chocolate filling and chocolate topping
truly lives up to its wicked name.

INGREDIENTS

Serves 8–10

90 g/3 oz/6 tbsp butter or soft
   margarine
125 g/4 oz/$^2/_3$ cup caster (superfine)
   sugar
150 g/5 oz/$^3/_4$ cup light soft brown
   sugar
300 g/10 oz/$2^1/_2$ cups plain
   (all-purpose) flour
2 tsp bicarbonate of soda (baking soda)
2 tbsp cocoa powder

4 eggs
125 g/4 oz/4 squares dark chocolate,
   melted
1 tbsp black treacle (molasses)
1 tsp vanilla flavouring (extract)
200 ml/7 fl oz/$^7/_8$ cup milk

WHITE FUDGE ICING
  (FROSTING):
250 g/8 oz/8 squares white
   chocolate
75 g/$2^1/_2$ oz/$^1/_3$ cup butter

about 250 g/8 oz/$1^1/_3$ cups icing
   (confectioners') sugar, sifted

CHOCOLATE FUDGE ICING
  (FROSTING):
1 recipe quantity (see page 48) plus
   2 tbsp icing (confectioners') sugar

TO DECORATE:
icing (confectioners') sugar, sifted
approx 10 dark chocolate leaves
   (see page 36)

METHOD

1. Grease and line the bases of 3 × 23–25 cm/9–10 inch sandwich cake tins (layer pans) with non-stick baking parchment. Cream the butter and sugars together until light and fluffy. Sift together the flour, bicarbonate of soda (baking soda) and cocoa powder in a separate bowl.
2. Beat the eggs into the creamed mixture one at a time, following each with a spoonful of the flour mixture. Beat in the melted chocolate, treacle (molasses) and vanilla flavouring (extract).

3. Fold in the remaining flour mixture, alternating with the milk, until smooth. Divide between the tins (pans) and level with a palette knife (spatula). Bake in a preheated oven at 180°C/350°F/Gas Mark 4 for 25–30 minutes, or until well risen and firm to the touch. Invert on to wire racks,

strip off the parchment and leave to cool.

4. To make the white icing (frosting), melt the white chocolate and butter in a heatproof bowl over a pan of simmering water, then beat in 2 tablespoons of boiling water until the mixture is smooth. Remove from the heat and beat in sufficient icing (confectioners') sugar to give a thick spreading consistency. Quickly use the icing (frosting) to sandwich the 3 cakes together.
5. Make the chocolate topping (see page 48). Beat in the extra icing (confectioners') sugar and leave to cool until thick and on the point of setting. Spread quickly over the top of the cake, swirling attractively, and leave to set.
6. Sprinkle the top of the cake with icing (confectioners') sugar and decorate with the chocolate leaves.

CHOCOLATE FUDGE
Icing (Frosting)
& CHOCOLATE
Ganache

These delicious toppings are perfect for chocolate-lovers! Chocolate ganache in particular is perhaps the richest and most irresistible of all icings (frostings).

Chocolate Fudge Icing (Frosting):

A rich mixture that can be used to coat cakes when it is warm, or used as a filling if left to cool and then beaten until soft.

Chocolate Ganache:

Used while warm, this will cover a cake with a thick, glossy coat. If you want to use it as a filling or for piping, leave it to cool and then beat it thoroughly.

INGREDIENTS

Fills and covers 20 cm/8 inch cake

60 g/2 oz/¼ cup butter
3 tbsp milk

250 g/8 oz/1⅓ cups icing (confectioners') sugar, sifted
2 tbsp sifted cocoa powder

Fills and covers 20 cm/8 inch cake

175 g/6 oz/6 squares dark chocolate, broken into pieces
4 tbsp single (light) cream

60 g/2 oz/¼ cup butter, cut into cubes
2 egg yolks
1 tbsp brandy

METHOD

1. Melt the butter in a small saucepan with the milk.
2. Add the sugar and cocoa, and beat well until smooth and glossy.
3. Leave until tepid, then pour over the cake.

VARIATION
Coffee Fudge Icing (Frosting): Replace the cocoa powder with 2 teaspoons instant coffee granules.
White Fudge Icing (Frosting): Use 2 tablespoons milk, add 60 g/2 oz/2 squares white chocolate to the pan and omit the cocoa powder.

1. Put the chocolate into a small saucepan with the cream and heat gently until melted.
2. Leave to cool slightly, then beat in the butter gradually.
3. Beat in the egg yolks and brandy. Leave to cool slightly until firm, stirring occasionally.

CHOCOLATE
Decorations

Chocolate can be melted and made into a wide range of luscious-looking decorations that are really quite easy to achieve. However, care must be taken when melting chocolate.

METHOD

TO MELT CHOCOLATE

1. Break some chocolate into small pieces and place in a heatproof bowl that fits snugly over a saucepan of water. Bring the water to the boil, turn off the heat and leave until the chocolate has melted. If it is overheated or if any steam or water comes into contact with the chocolate, it will become stiff and granular and lose its smooth glossiness.
2. Alternatively, put the chocolate in a heatproof bowl and place in a microwave oven at Full Power for 2 minutes, stirring occasionally.

TO MAKE CHOCOLATE SHAPES

1. Spread a thin layer of melted chocolate on to baking parchment and leave until set but not too hard.
2. Cut out shapes with cutters or a sharp knife. Pipe a different colour of chocolate on the shapes to decorate.

DIPPED FRUIT AND NUTS

1. Add 1–2 teaspoons vegetable oil, or more if necessary, to the melted chocolate to make it more fluid.
2. Half-dip fruits such as strawberries, grapes or Cape gooseberries (ground cherries), drain off as much chocolate as possible and place on baking parchment to set. Walnuts, almonds and Brazil nuts can also be dipped.

PIPED CHOCOLATE

1. Pour melted chocolate into a baking parchment piping bag (pastry bag) and leave to cool slightly so the consistency is not too thin. Snip off the end and pipe zigzag lines.

CHOCOLATE CURLS

1. Scrape a potato peeler across a block of chocolate. The chocolate should not be too cold or the curls will break into small pieces.

GRATED CHOCOLATE

1. Use a coarse grater and make sure the chocolate and your hands are cold. Keep turning the chocolate as you grate, to prevent the side you are holding from melting.

CHOCOLATE LEAVES

To make chocolate leaves, see page 36.

TIPS

There is a wide variety of piping tubes and bags available. A couple of medium-size piping bags (pastry bags) and a few straight line writing tubes and star nozzles (tips) should be enough to pipe messages and simple decorations. Alternatively, simply make a cone shape out of a sheet of baking parchment and snip off the end (as above).

FRUIT
Bites

These chocolate-dipped bonbons can be made as gifts or served with coffee as after-dinner treats. Cherries, dates and Cape gooseberries (ground cherries) are used here, but other fruits will do just as well.

INGREDIENTS

Makes 32

8 fresh cherries with stalks
2 tbsp kirsch or brandy

8 large dates
350 g/12 oz white marzipan (almond paste)
8 Cape gooseberries (ground cherries)

175 g/6 oz/6 squares dark chocolate
60 g/2 oz toasted hazelnuts or almonds, very finely chopped
8 kumquats

METHOD

1. If you can't find liqueur-soaked cherries, make your own by piercing fresh cherries with a darning needle in several places and soaking them in the kirsch or brandy for 24 hours. Drain thoroughly on paper towels.

2. Cut the dates along the top and ease out the stones (pits). Use a little of the marzipan (almond paste) to fill the centres of the dates evenly.

3. Using a large piece of non-stick baking parchment to work on, roll out some of the marzipan (almond paste) thinly and cut out 8 × 6 cm/2½ inch rounds with a fluted cutter. Place a cherry in the centre of each round and enclose, pinching the marzipan (almond paste) around the cherry stalk to make a neat pouch.

4. Open up the papery leaves of the Cape gooseberries (ground cherries) to reveal all of the orange-coloured fruit. Then cut 8 slightly smaller fluted rounds out of the marzipan (almond paste) and mould these around the Cape gooseberries (ground cherries) so that the top third

is left uncovered.

5. Melt the chocolate in a heatproof bowl set over a saucepan of gently simmering water or place in a microwave set on Full Power for about 3 minutes until melted. Dip the bottom half of each Cape gooseberry (ground cherry) in the chocolate so there is still a line of marzipan (almond paste) left uncovered, shake off any excess chocolate then dip just the base in the chopped nuts and stand on a sheet of non-stick baking parchment. Do the same with the cherries so half the marzipan (almond paste) is covered, then dip half of the cherries in the nuts, leaving the other 4 plain. Dip the bottom two-thirds of each kumquat into the chocolate.

6. Dip a pastry brush in the remaining melted chocolate and paint a thick strip of chocolate over the centre of the dates, including the marzipan (almond paste), and sprinkle with nuts. Leave to set with the other fruits. To serve, either place on a doyley on a small plate or serve in paper petit fours cases.

CHILDREN'S CHOCOLATE CHOICE

Practically every child loves chocolate, and the ways in which it can be presented are unlimited. Children will devour almost anything that is chocolate-flavoured and they find it great fun if they can help in the kitchen too.

Chocolate ice cream is a popular favourite, but it is made even better when a rich chocolate sauce is spooned over. Milk shakes are not only delicious but encourage children to drink more milk and together with the ice cream give a new dimension to a daily pinta. (For adults a tablespoon or two of rum makes the ice cream even better!) The moist sponge Chocolate Butterfly Cakes and crisp Chocolate Chip Cookies are very moreish and are suitable for snacks and picnic boxes as well as teatime treats; and the Chocolate Refrigerator Cake comes in many guises from a quick biscuity snack to a fairly ornate dessert. Don't forget to try the Chocolate Nests – they may look a little tricky but are really very simple once the cereal has been coated in the melted chocolate, and they will delight many a child.

CHOCOLATE
Nests

*This is a scrumptious Easter treat for children and it's so easy to
make that they can help to prepare them in the kitchen.*

INGREDIENTS

Makes 4

176 g/6 oz/6 squares dark chocolate

60 g/2 oz/^{1}/4 cup butter
3 cereal biscuits, such as Shredded
   Wheat

60 g/2 oz/^{1}/3 cup raisins
18–24 miniature chocolate or other
   candy eggs

METHOD

1. Lightly grease a
   4 individual Yorkshire
   puddings tray
   (muffin pan).
2. Melt the chocolate
   and butter in a
   heatproof bowl over a
   saucepan of gently
   simmering water until
   smooth, making sure
   no water splashes
   into the chocolate. Alternatively, heat in a microwave set
   on Full Power for about 3 minutes until melted.
3. Crumble the cereal biscuits and stir them into the
   melted chocolate with the raisins so they are completely
   coated in chocolate.

4. Carefully spoon the mixture into the tins to represent
   nests and make a depression in the centre of each 'nest'
   with the back of a
   spoon. Leave to chill
   until set.
5. Carefully remove
   each set chocolate
   nest and fill with
   miniature chocolate
   eggs. When they are
   not available in the
   shops they can be
   made by mixing
   marzipan (almond
   paste) with sifted
   cocoa powder and shaping the mixture into small eggs.

CHOCOLATE NESTS
*The nest effect used here is simply achieved by using crumbled up breakfast
cereal biscuits dipped in melted chocolate. The effect is amazingly realistic.
Don't reserve this recipe until Easter as they make delightful party treats.*

CHOCOLATE REFRIGERATOR *Cake*

As there is no cooking involved in making this cake, it is easy and fun for children to make and yet it is an impressive-looking dessert. The brandy is for adult's only!

INGREDIENTS

Serves 8–10

350 g/12 oz/12 squares dark chocolate

8 tbsp black coffee (or 4 tbsp coffee and 4 tbsp brandy)

250 g/8 oz digestive biscuits (graham crackers), roughly crushed

90 g/3 oz/1 cup toasted flaked (slivered) almonds

90 g/3 oz/^{1}/$_3$ cup glacé (candied) cherries

300 ml/^{1}/$_2$ pint/1^1/$_4$ cups double (heavy) cream

8–10 Cape gooseberries (ground

cherries) or chocolate drops (optional)

CHOCOLATE CARAQUE:
90 g/3 oz/3 squares dark chocolate, broken into pieces

METHOD

1. Grease an 18 cm/7 inch round loose-based cake tin (pan). Melt the chocolate with the coffee in a heatproof bowl placed over a saucepan of gently simmering water, making sure the bowl does not touch the bottom of the pan and that no water splashes into the chocolate.

2. When melted, remove the chocolate from the heat and stir in the brandy (if using), crushed biscuits (crackers), almonds and glacé (candied) cherries until evenly blended.

3. Pour the mixture into the prepared tin (pan) and smooth the top. Leave to cool and then chill thoroughly in the refrigerator, preferably overnight.

4. Carefully remove from the cake tin (pan) and turn on to a serving plate. Whip the cream until stiff and either spread a thin layer over the top of the cake and then decorate with piped whirls of cream, or simply decorate with whirls of cream. Complete the decoration with

Cape gooseberries (ground cherries), chocolate drops or chocolate caraque (see below). Alternatively, just cut into wedges and serve.

5. To make chocolate caraque, melt the chocolate in a heatproof bowl set over a pan of gently simmering water or in a microwave set on Full Power for 1–1^1/$_2$ minutes. Using a palette knife (spatula), spread the melted chocolate thinly over a cool flat surface, such as marble, and then leave until just on the point of setting – it must be firm but not hard.

6. Either push a sharp knife held at a 45° angle over the surface, scraping off long scrolls of chocolate, or pare off the chocolate with a cheese slice. When it becomes too hard, melt the chocolate again, then repeat the process on a clean surface. Store the caraque between layers of baking parchment in a rigid container and keep in the refrigerator or other cool place for up to 2–3 weeks.

CHOCOLATE
Butterfly Cakes

Sponge cakes of any flavour can be used, but here both the sponge and the butter cream filling are chocolate-flavoured to satisfy every chocolate-lover's appetite!

INGREDIENTS

Makes 16

125 g/4 oz/^{1}/$_2$ cup butter or margarine

125 g/4 oz/^{2}/$_3$ cup caster (superfine) sugar

2 eggs, beaten

100g/3^1/$_2$ oz/^{3}/$_4$ cup plus 1 tbsp self-raising flour, sifted

1^1/$_2$ tbsp cocoa powder, sifted

large pinch of baking powder

1 tbsp water

a few drops of vanilla flavouring (extract)

icing (confectioner's) sugar, for dredging

BUTTER CREAM:

125 g/4 oz/^{1}/$_2$ cup butter (preferably unsalted)

250 g/8 oz/1^3/$_4$ cups icing (confectioners') sugar, sifted

2 tbsp cocoa powder, sifted

1–2 tbsp milk

a few drops of vanilla flavouring (extract)

a little coarsely grated chocolate (optional)

METHOD

1. Cream the butter or margarine and sugar together until very light, fluffy and pale in colour. Beat in the eggs, one at a time, following each with a spoonful of the sifted flour. Fold in the remaining flour with the cocoa and baking powder, followed by the water and vanilla flavouring (extract).

2. Line 16 patty tins with paper cake cases or grease them thoroughly and dredge lightly with flour. Divide the cake mixture between the paper cases.

3. Bake in a preheated oven at 190°C/375°F/Gas Mark 5

for 15–20 minutes or until well risen and just firm to the touch. Turn out on to a wire rack and leave to cool.

4. To make the butter cream, cream the butter until soft and then beat in the sugar and cocoa powder with sufficient milk until smooth enough to give a piping consistency. Add the vanilla flavouring (extract). Place in a piping bag (pastry bag) fitted with a small star nozzle (tip).

5. Cut a small piece out of the top of each sponge cake, leaving about 1 cm/^{1}/$_2$ inch all round the top surface uncut; and then cut the removed piece in half to form the 'wings'.

6. Pipe a whirl of butter cream to fill the hole which has been cut out of each sponge cake. Place the 'wings' in position, tilting them up at the edges. Either leave the 'wings' as they are or pipe a little butter cream between and/or around them. Dredge lightly with sifted icing (confectioners') sugar, if liked, or sprinkle over a few pieces of coarsely grated chocolate before serving.

CHOCOLATE CHIP
Cookies

Making cookies is easy, and the kitchen will smell wonderful!
These chocolate cookies won't hang around for long as they are extremely moreish.

INGREDIENTS

Makes 20

90 g/3 oz/6 tbsp butter
200 g/6½ oz/1 cup soft dark brown
    sugar
½ tsp vanilla flavouring (extract)

1 egg, beaten
175 g/6 oz/1½ cups self-raising flour
pinch of salt
60 g/2 oz/½ cup shelled walnuts,
    chopped
90 g/3 oz/½ cup chocolate cooking

dots or chocolate buttons
a little icing (confectioners') sugar,
    for dredging (optional)

METHOD

1. Cream the butter, sugar and vanilla flavouring (extract) until thick and fluffy; then beat in the egg gradually until well blended.

2. Sift the flour and salt together and fold into the mixture with the walnuts. Add the chocolate dots or buttons and mix well.

3. Place spoonfuls of the mixture well spaced out on greased baking sheets lined with non-stick baking parchment. Bake in a preheated oven at 180°C/350°F/Gas Mark 4 for about 15 minutes until firm and lightly coloured.

4. Leave the cookies on the baking sheets for a few minutes before transferring them carefully to wire racks. When cooled store in an airtight container in a cool place. Before serving, the cookies may be lightly dredged with icing (confectioners')

sugar, if liked. Other ingredients such as raisins or currants, chopped crystallized ginger or glacé (candied) cherries can be added with the chocolate, as can the finely grated zest of half an orange to ring the changes.

CHOCOLATE
Pancakes

Impossible to resist until Shrove Tuesday, these pancakes will prove to be a very popular treat.
Real chocoholics can add even more melted chocolate to the batter.

INGREDIENTS

Serves 4–8

125 g/4 oz/1 cup plain (all-purpose) flour
pinch of salt
2 eggs
275 ml/9 fl oz/1$^{1}/_{8}$ cup milk

100 g/3$^{1}/_{2}$ oz/3$^{1}/_{2}$ squares dark chocolate, melted
1 level tbsp caster (superfine) sugar
2 tbsp melted butter, lard or oil
250–500 g/$^{1}/_{2}$–1 lb/1$^{1}/_{2}$–3 cups fresh or frozen raspberries
mint sprigs, to garnish

CUSTARD:
600 ml/1 pint/2$^{1}/_{2}$ cups milk
90 g/3 oz/$^{1}/_{2}$ cup caster (superfine) sugar
1 tbsp plain (all-purpose) flour
6 egg yolks or 3 eggs and 3 egg yolks

METHOD

1. Sift the flour and salt into a bowl and make a well in the centre. Add the eggs and a little of the milk and gradually whisk in the flour from the sides, adding up to half the milk, until smooth. Whisk in the rest of the milk until smooth, then beat in the melted chocolate and sugar until evenly blended.

2. Brush a small frying pan (skillet) or pancake pan with a little of the melted butter, lard or oil. Holding the pan over a medium heat, tilt it to one side and add about 2 tablespoons of the chocolate pancake batter. Immediately tilt the pan in the other direction so that the batter coats the base of the pan.

3. Cook for about 1 minute then loosen the pancake, turn over and cook for 1 minute, ensuring that the pancake doesn't burn or overbrown. Transfer to a serving plate. Make 7 more pancakes in the same way, stacking them up on the plate with a disc of baking parchment between each pancake. Cover completely with foil and keep warm.

4. To make the custard, bring the milk just to boiling point so the surface shimmers and then remove from the heat. Whisk together the sugar, flour and eggs in a bowl until pale in colour then gradually whisk in the hot milk.

5. Return the mixture to a clean pan and cook over a low heat, stirring constantly until the mixture thickens. Do not let it boil or it will curdle. Strain the custard.

6. To serve, spoon a little custard on to individual serving plates. Fold the pancakes into quarters, tuck some raspberries into the centre of each and place on top of the custard. Pour over a little more custard and serve warm, decorated with mint sprigs.

CHOCOLATE
Ice Cream

Everyone loves a good chocolate ice cream, and this is the real thing! Add nuts, peppermint, chocolate chips and so on according to taste or simply enjoy the pure chocolate taste.

INGREDIENTS

Serves 4–6

300 ml/$^1/_2$ pint/1$^1/_4$ cups milk
90 g/3 oz/$^1/_2$ cup caster (superfine) sugar

2 eggs
2 egg yolks
1 tsp vanilla flavouring (extract)
125 g/4 oz/4 squares dark chocolate, broken up

300 ml/$^1/_2$ pint/1$^1/_4$ cups double (heavy) cream
coarsely pared curls of luxury dark chocolate (see page 50), for decoration (optional)

METHOD

1. Gently heat the milk and sugar together in a pan. Beat the eggs and yolks together in a bowl and pour on to the warm milk, stirring constantly. Strain the mixture into a heatproof bowl and set over a saucepan of gently simmering water. Cook, stirring continuously, until the custard thickens enough to coat the back of a spoon. Stir in the vanilla flavouring (extract).

2. Melt the chocolate in a heatproof bowl set over a pan of gently simmering water, making sure the water doesn't splash into the bowl. Alternatively, heat in a microwave oven set on Full Power for 2 minutes, stirring once halfway through.

3. Stir the melted chocolate into the custard until evenly blended, then cover with cling film (plastic wrap) and leave until cold.

4. Whip the cream until very thick but not stiff and fold evenly into the cold chocolate custard mixture. Turn into a shallow container, cover with cling film (plastic wrap) and freeze until partially frozen; that is, until the ice crystals reach at least 2.5 cm/1 inch in from the side of the container.

5. Turn the ice cream into a cold bowl and whisk hard, preferably using a hand-held electric mixer, until the ice crystals are completely broken down and the ice cream is smooth. Return to a suitable freezing container, cover again and freeze until firm.

6. Remove the ice cream from the freezer and transfer to the refrigerator for at least 30 minutes before serving or leave at room temperature for 10–20 minutes to allow it to soften slightly and make it easier to serve. Serve decorated with chocolate curls in small bowls or glasses.

VARIATIONS
Add one of the following when whisking the ice cream to break down the ice crystals:
4 tablespoons of toasted chopped hazelnuts or almonds; 4–6 tablespoons of coarsely grated or chopped dark, milk or white chocolate; or 4 tablespoons of crushed chocolate mint crisps, coffee crisps or orange crisps.
For mocha ice cream, add 1 tablespoon of coffee flavouring (extract) with the vanilla flavouring (extract).

CHOCOLATE CHIP
Ice Cream

*This frozen dessert offers the best of both worlds – delicious cookies
and a rich dairy-flavoured ice cream.*

INGREDIENTS

Serves 6

300 ml/^{1}/$_2$ pint/1^1/$_4$ cups milk
1 vanilla pod (bean)

2 eggs
2 egg yolks
60 g/2 oz/^{1}/$_4$ cup caster (superfine)
    sugar

300 ml/^{1}/$_2$ pint/1^1/$_4$ cups natural yogurt
125 g/4 oz Chocolate Chip Cookies,
    broken into small pieces (see
    page 62).

METHOD

1. Pour the milk into a small pan, add the vanilla pod (bean) and bring slowly to the boil. Remove from the heat, cover the pan and leave to cool.

2. Beat the eggs and egg yolks in a double boiler, or in a bowl over a pan of simmering water. Add the sugar and continue beating until the mixture is pale and creamy.

3. Reheat the milk to simmering point and strain it over the egg mixture. Stir continuously until the custard is thick enough to coat the back of a spoon. Remove the custard from the heat and stand the pan or bowl in cold water to prevent any further cooking. Wash and dry the vanilla pod (bean) to store for future use. See below for advice on vanilla pods (beans).

4. Stir the yogurt into the cooled custard and beat until it is well blended. When the mixture is thoroughly cold, stir in the broken cookies.

5. Transfer the mixture to a chilled metal cake tin (pan) or polythene container, cover and freeze for 4 hours. Remove from the freezer every hour, transfer to a chilled bowl and beat vigorously to prevent ice crystals forming. Alternatively, freeze the mixture in an ice-cream maker, following the manufacturer's instructions.

6. To serve the ice cream, transfer it to the main part of the refrigerator for at least 30 minutes. Serve in scoops.

VANILLA PODS (BEANS)
*Vanilla pods (beans) can be used to flavour any hot liquid.
For a stronger flavour, split the pod lengthwise with a sharp knife before
infusing it in the hot liquid for 20–30 minutes. For a very strong flavour,
scrape the seeds out of the pod and add to the liquid when infusing.
Rinse and dry the pod after use. It can be stored in a jar of sugar,
to which it will impart its flavour.*

ICED CHOCOLATE
Milk Shake

*If you keep a batch of the rich chocolate sauce in the refrigerator,
these delicious shakes can be whipped up in seconds. A lighter version can be made with
low-fat ice cream and semi-skimmed milk. Omit the rum for the children!*

INGREDIENTS

Serves 4

900 ml/1½ pints/3½ cups cold milk
4 scoops chocolate ice cream (see
    page 66)

1 tsp cocoa powder

RICH CHOCOLATE SAUCE:
250 g/8 oz/8 squares bitter
    (semisweet) chocolate

2 tbsp golden (light corn) syrup
2 tbsp coffee flavouring (extract)
300 ml/½ pint/1¼ cups single (light)
    cream
2 tbsp dark rum (optional)

METHOD

1. To make the chocolate sauce, break the chocolate into pieces and place into a heavy-based saucepan. Add the syrup, coffee flavouring (extract) and cream. Cook over a low heat, stirring, until smooth and glossy.

2. Stir in the rum, if using, and leave to cool. The sauce will thicken as it cools. Store in an airtight container in the refrigerator for up to 1 week. Stir to mix well or heat gently before serving.

3. Whisk the cold milk and 150 ml/¼ pint/ ⅔ cup of the rich chocolate sauce together vigorously, or place in a blender until the liquid is frothy and well blended.

4. Pour the mixture into 4 tall (preferably chilled) glasses and then place a scoop of chocolate ice cream carefully on top so that it floats.

5. Dust the top of each milk shake with a little sifted cocoa powder. Serve at once.

VARIATIONS
*Vanilla or chocolate chip or minted ice cream can be used in this milk shake.
Chopped toasted hazelnuts or almonds can be sprinkled over
the top just before serving.*

DINNER-PARTY DESSERTS

What to serve your guests for dessert is always a difficult decision to make when you are planning a dinner party. However, you can't go far wrong if you choose a recipe containing chocolate. It can feature plain, milk or white chocolate or a combination of these, but whatever you pick should be easy to make in advance with only final simple decorations necessary at the last minute, or a very easy creation which only takes a few minutes to prepare and complete.

A meringue gâteau with a rich chocolate filling and grated chocolate topping will provide irresistible temptation; a chocolate terrine with layers of both white and dark chocolate will make a smooth and surprisingly light finish to a meal; and an orange-flavoured gâteau topped with masses of caraque chocolate curls to grace any table.

These are only three of the luscious and mouth-watering desserts featured in this chapter which will help turn all your dinner parties into memorable feasts.

CHOCOLATE FLOWER
Gâteau

A luscious-looking cake that requires practice and a bit of patience. The chocolate cones can be made in advance and stored in an airtight container until you need them.

INGREDIENTS

Makes 20 cm/8 inch gâteau

3-egg chocolate-flavoured Whisked Sponge Cake mixture (see page 95)

1 quantity Chocolate Ganache (see page 48)

250 g/8 oz/8 squares chocolate, melted

icing (confectioners') sugar for dredging

METHOD

1. Grease a 20 cm/8 inch deep cake tin (pan) and line with baking parchment. Turn the mixture into the tin (pan) and bake in a preheated oven at 190°/375°F/Gas Mark 5 for 30 minutes until the cake springs back when lightly pressed. Invert on a wire rack to cool.

2. Cut the cake in half horizontally and sandwich together with one third of the chocolate ganache. Spread more ganache over the top and sides of the cake.

3. Cut a band of baking parchment slightly longer than the circumference of the cake and a little deeper. Spread thickly with melted chocolate and leave until set, but not brittle. Trim the chocolate to the exact size of the cake.

4. Lift the baking parchment and attach the chocolate to the side of the cake, easing it gently round to cover the ganache, then peel off the paper.

5. Spread more melted chocolate on to a marble slab or other cold surface, using a palette knife (spatula), and leave to set.

6. When it is just set, push a sharp knife held at a 45° angle over the surface to scrape it into cones (see below). Arrange these on the top of the cake, starting from the outside and working to the centre, placing the cones in overlapping layers to resemble a flower. Dredge with icing (confectioners') sugar.

CHOCOLATE CONES
To make successful cones, the chocolate must be at just the right temperature. If it is not set enough it will not form a curl as you scrape. If the chocolate becomes too hard, it will crack as you scrape it off.

ORANGE CARAQUE
Gâteau

An oblong orange-flavoured cake with a rich orange filling, a masking of chocolate butter cream and a topping of caraque chocolate.

INGREDIENTS

Serves 8–10

175 g/6 oz/³/₄ cup butter or soft margarine
90 g/3 oz/¹/₃ cup caster (superfine) sugar
90 g/3 oz/¹/₂ cup light soft brown sugar

3 eggs
175 g/6 oz/1¹/₂ cups self-raising flour, sifted
grated zest of 1 large orange
3 tbsp orange juice
4 tbsp orange-flavoured liqueur
1 quantity Orange Pastry Cream (see page 94)

1 tsp orange flower water
grated zest of ¹/₂–1 orange
250 g/8 oz/8 squares dark chocolate
1 quantity Chocolate Butter Cream (see page 94)
icing (confectioners') sugar for dredging

METHOD

1. Grease a rectangular tin (pan), about 28 × 18 × 4 cm/ 11 × 7 × 1¹/₂ inches, and line with non-stick baking parchment. Make the cake as for Victoria Sandwich (Sponge Layer Cake) (see page 94), adding the orange zest and using 1 tablespoon of the orange juice instead of the water. Spoon into the tin (pan), level the top and bake in a preheated oven at 190°C/375°F/Gas Mark 5 for 25–30 minutes, or until well risen and firm to the touch.

2. Invert the cake on a wire rack and leave to cool, then peel off the baking parchment. Combine the remaining orange juice with the liqueur and sprinkle over the cake.

3. Simmer the orange pastry cream for 1 minute, then remove from the heat and beat in the orange flower water and orange zest. Cover with clingfilm (plastic wrap) and leave until cold.

4. Cut the cake in half lengthways to give 2 slabs and sandwich together with the orange pastry cream.

5. Use 90–125 g/3–4 oz/ 3–4 squares of the chocolate to make chocolate curls (see page 50). Use the remaining chocolate to make chocolate caraque (see page 58).

6. Cover the whole cake with the chocolate butter cream and then use the chocolate curls to cover the sides of the gâteau. Arrange the caraque along the top of the gâteau and then dust lightly with icing (confectioners') sugar before serving.

CHOCOLATE TRUFFLE
Cheesecake

The combination of flavours that are built up through the layers, from almond through coffee to chocolate, make this dessert a truly memorable experience.

INGREDIENTS

Serves 8

60 g/2 oz/¼ cup unsalted butter
125 g/4 oz Amaretti biscuits (cookies), crushed
250 g/8 oz low-fat soft cheese
250 g/8 oz mascarpone
150 ml/¼ pint/⅔ cup crème fraîche
½ tsp vanilla flavouring (extract)

90 g/3 oz/½ cup golden caster (superfine) sugar
2 eggs, plus 1 egg yolk
1 tbsp flour
1 tbsp instant coffee granules
125 ml/4 fl oz/½ cup boiling water
2 tbsp coffee liqueur, or brandy
7 sponge fingers (boudoir biscuits)

TOPPING:
15 g/½ oz/1 tbsp unsalted butter
150 ml/¼ pint/⅔ cup natural yogurt
60 g/2 oz/⅓ cup golden caster (superfine) sugar
125 g/4 oz/4 squares plain chocolate, broken up
1 tbsp coffee liqueur or brandy
1 tbsp cocoa powder

METHOD

1. Grease and line an 18 cm/7 inch loose-bottomed cake tin (pan). Melt the butter in a small pan over low heat. Remove from the heat, stir in the crushed Amaretti biscuits (cookies) and tip them into the prepared tin (pan). Press the crushed biscuits (cookies) to cover the base evenly and chill.

2. Beat together the soft cheese, mascarpone, crème fraîche and vanilla. Beat in the sugar, eggs, egg yolk and flour. Pour half into the tin (pan).

3. Dissolve the coffee in the boiling water, add the liqueur and pour into a small bowl. Quickly dip the sponge fingers (boudoir biscuits) into the coffee. Arrange them over the cheese mixture and spoon on the remaining cheese mixture.

4. Bake in a preheated oven at 200°C/400°F/Gas Mark 6 for 20 minutes, then lower the heat to 140°C/275°F/Gas Mark 1 and cook for a further 1½ hours, or until a skewer inserted into the centre of the cake comes out clean. Allow the cake to cool before removing from the tin (pan).

5. To make the topping, bring the butter, yogurt and sugar to the boil. Add the chocolate and liqueur and stir over a low heat for 2–3 minutes. Remove from the heat and beat to blend thoroughly. Leave until completely cold, then spoon the mixture into a piping bag and pipe lines or squiggles over the top of the cheesecake. Just before serving, dust the top with cocoa powder.

DOUBLE CHOCOLATE
Terrine

This blend of white and dark chocolate mousse laced with rum, set in a loaf tin (pan) for easy carriage and serving, is finished with a fresh raspberry coulis and fresh raspberries.

INGREDIENTS

Serves 6–8

WHITE CHOCOLATE MOUSSE:
250 g/8 oz/8 squares white chocolate
1¹/₂ tsp powdered gelatine plus 2 tbsp water
2 tbsp caster (superfine) sugar
2 egg yolks
150 ml/¹/₄ pint/²/₃ cup soured cream
150 ml/¹/₄ pint/²/₃ cup double (heavy) cream, whipped until thick

DARK CHOCOLATE MOUSSE:
175 g/6 oz/6 squares dark chocolate
2 tbsp black coffee (not too strong)
2 tsp powdered gelatine plus 1 tbsp water
2 tbsp rum
60 g/2 oz/¹/₄ cup butter, softened
2 egg yolks
300 ml/¹/₂ pint/1¹/₄ cups double (heavy) cream, whipped

RASPBERRY COULIS:
175 g/6 oz/1 cup fresh or frozen raspberries
about 1 tbsp icing (confectioners') sugar

TO DECORATE:
whipped cream
chocolate curls (see page 50)

METHOD

1. Line a 23 × 12 cm/9 × 5 inch loaf tin (pan) with cling film (plastic wrap), leaving plenty of overhang.
2. To make the white chocolate mousse, break up the chocolate and melt in a bowl, either in a microwave oven on Full Power for about 3¹/₂ minutes or over a pan of gently simmering water. Remove from the heat and stir until smooth.

3. Dissolve the gelatine in the water in a bowl set over a pan of simmering water. Leave to cool slightly, then beat into the chocolate with the sugar and egg yolks, and then the soured cream. Fold in the double (heavy) cream. Pour into the tin (pan) and chill until set.

4. To make the dark chocolate mousse, melt the chocolate with the coffee. Dissolve the gelatine in the rum with the water, as in step 3. Stir the dissolved gelatine into the melted chocolate, then add the butter. Stir until blended then beat in the egg yolks. Fold the cream into the mousse. Pour over the white chocolate mousse and chill until set.

5. To make the coulis, sieve (strain) the raspberries and sweeten to taste with the sugar. Turn the terrine out, peel off the cling film (plastic wrap) and decorate with whipped cream and chocolate curls. Spoon the coulis around the base to serve.

WHITE CHOCOLATE
Pots

*A delicious white chocolate and rum mousse, which is only softly set
and is flavoured with fromage frais.*

INGREDIENTS

Serves 2

90 g/3 oz/3 squares white chocolate
15 g/¹/₂ oz/1 tbsp butter

1 tbsp rum
1 egg, separated
1 tbsp natural fromage frais

TO DECORATE:
whipped cream or natural fromage
   frais
fresh raspberries (optional)
fresh mint leaves

METHOD

1. Break up the white chocolate and put into a heatproof
bowl with the butter. Place over a saucepan of very
gently simmering water, and heat gently until completely melted, stirring frequently.

2. Remove the bowl from the heat and beat in the rum, followed by the egg yolk and finally the fromage frais. Leave to cool.

3. Whisk the egg white until very stiff and dry and fold evenly through the white chocolate mixture.

4. Divide between 2 individual serving pots and chill until set. This mousse does not set very firmly.

5. Before serving, top each pot with a spoonful of whipped cream or fromage frais and decorate with a few raspberries and fresh mint leaves. Alternatively, sprinkle with some grated dark chocolate, or a chocolate flake bar, roughly crumbled.

VARIATION
*For a variation, 1–2 tablespoons of coarsely grated chocolate can be folded
through the mixture with the egg white or dark chocolate may be used instead
of white chocolate. The grated zest of ¹/₂ small orange may also be added to
give an orange flavouring.*

BRANDY MOCHA
Cups

*A very rich and delicious chocolate dessert that literally takes minutes to make,
although you do have to wait for it to set.*

INGREDIENTS

Serves: 4

250 ml/8 fl oz/1 cup double (heavy)
   cream
1 tsp coffee granules

125 g/4 oz/4 squares dark chocolate,
   broken into pieces
2 tbsp brandy
75 ml/3 fl oz/$^1/_3$ cup double (heavy)
   cream

chocolate curls (see page 50) to
   decorate
Amaretti biscuits (cookies) to serve

METHOD

1. Put the cream, coffee and chocolate into a saucepan and heat gently over a low heat, stirring occasionally, until the chocolate has completely melted.
2. Add the brandy to the chocolate and coffee mixture in the saucepan and stir well until completely smooth. Remove the saucepan from the heat and set aside to cool completely.

3. Pour the cooled chocolate and brandy mixture into 4 individual glass serving dishes and leave to chill in the refrigerator until completely set.
4. Pile a generous spoonful of cream on top of each brandy mocha cup. Decorate with a sprinkling of chocolate curls (see page 50) and serve with a few Amaretti biscuits (cookies).

VARIATIONS
*You can use all kinds of flavourings in this delicious dessert.
Try replacing the brandy with almond liqueur to enhance the
flavour of the Amaretti biscuits (cookies). Alternatively, use
cherry brandy or orange liqueur, both of which work extremely
well with the richness of the chocolate.
For a completely non-alcoholic version, substitute orange juice
for the brandy and decorate with a little grated orange zest.*

HOT MOCHA
Soufflé

Soufflés are not difficult to make, provided your recipe is reliable. The chocolate sauce used here is a delightful addition to the recipe.

INGREDIENTS

Serves 6

butter for greasing
2 tbsp caster (superfine) sugar
2 egg yolks
3 tsp icing (confectioners') sugar
2 tsp plain (all-purpose) flour

150 g/5 oz/5 squares dark chocolate, melted
2 tsp instant coffee powder, dissolved in 1 tbsp hot water
4 egg whites
icing (confectioners') sugar, to decorate

SAUCE:
60 g/2 oz/¹/₃ cup granulated sugar
50 ml/2 fl oz/¹/₄ cup water
100 g/3¹/₂ oz/3¹/₂ squares dark chocolate
1 tbsp instant coffee powder
75 ml/3 fl oz/¹/₃ cup whipping cream

METHOD

1. Grease a 900 ml/1¹/₂ pint/3¹/₂ cup soufflé dish. Dust with the caster (superfine) sugar and tap out any excess.
2. Wrap a piece of baking parchment around the soufflé

dish, to twice the depth of the dish. Secure with string or an elastic band.
3. Beat the egg yolks until pale and sift in the icing (confectioners') sugar.
4. Stir in the flour, melted chocolate and coffee.
5. Whisk the egg whites until just stiff and fold into the soufflé mixture.
6. Pour the mixture into the soufflé dish right up to the rim. Run the tip of a knife between the soufflé and the edge of the dish. Bake

in a preheated oven at 180°C/350°F/Gas Mark 4 for 45 minutes (do not open the oven door during cooking time).
7. To make the sauce, put the sugar and water into a saucepan. Simmer until dissolved, then add the chocolate, coffee powder and cream. Keep warm until ready to serve.
8. To serve, transfer the sauce to a warmed serving jug and, working quickly, remove the parchment from the soufflé dish, dust the soufflé with the icing (confectioners') sugar and transfer to the table before it sinks. Make a hole in the top of the soufflé with a knife, and pour in the sauce, preferably from a great height!

CHOCOLATE
Coconut Layer

This is a rich, easy dessert for chocolate-lovers. If you can't wait, it can be eaten straightaway, still warm and gooey, or it can be chilled until set and served with coffee.

INGREDIENTS

Serves 6–8

200 g/7 oz/7 squares dark chocolate, broken into pieces
300 g/10 oz/1¼ cups full-fat soft cheese

60 g/2 oz/²/₃ cup grated or desiccated (shredded) coconut
250 g/8 oz/2 cups digestive biscuits (graham crackers), crumbled

TO DECORATE:
icing (confectioners') sugar
coconut curls or desiccated (shredded) coconut

METHOD

1. Melt the chocolate in a heatproof bowl set over a saucepan of barely simmering water for 10 minutes. Do not let the water splash into the bowl, as it will affect the texture of the chocolate.

2. Turn off the heat. Add the soft cheese to the melted chocolate and stir until well blended and smooth.
3. Stir in the grated or desiccated (shredded) coconut.
4. Place half of the biscuit (cracker) crumbs on the bottom of a shallow 1.1 litre/ 2 pint/4½ cup dish.

5. Layer with half the chocolate mixture, then another layer of the remaining biscuit (cracker) crumbs, finishing with a layer of the remaining chocolate mixture. Chill for 2 hours.
6. Dust with icing (confectioners') sugar and decorate with coconut curls or desiccated (shredded) coconut before serving.

COCONUT CURLS
If using a fresh coconut, drain the milk and split the coconut apart using a hammer. Remove the flesh from the shell in large pieces. To make the curls, peel down one side of each piece of coconut flesh with a peeler and use the resulting curls for decoration.

TIPS
This can be kept for up to 5 days in the refrigerator but remember to cover the dish carefully so that the dessert doesn't absorb other flavours.
If you prefer, you can make individual desserts using 6–8 ramekins or glasses instead of one large bowl. Distribute the ingredients evenly among the ramekins.

CHOCOLATE MERINGUE
Gâteau

Layers of meringue with a chocolate crème pâtissière and cream filling
topped with chocolate and nuts make this the perfect dessert for a special occasion.

INGREDIENTS

Serves 8–10

5 egg whites
300 g/10 oz/1¹/₂ cups caster
  (superfine) sugar
150 ml/¹/₄ pint/²/₃ cup double (heavy)
  cream
60 g/2 oz/2 squares dark chocolate,
  grated or in curls

toasted hazelnuts (optional)
whole strawberries (optional)

FILLING:
300 ml/¹/₂ pint/1¹/₄ cups milk
60 g/2 oz/¹/₃ cup caster (superfine)
  sugar
30 g/1 oz/¹/₄ cup plain (all-purpose)
  flour

15 g/¹/₂ oz cornflour (cornstarch)
1 egg
1 egg yolk
a few drops of vanilla flavouring
  (extract)
60 g/2 oz/2 squares dark chocolate,
  melted
1–2 tbsp rum (optional)

METHOD

1. Draw a 20 cm/8 inch and a 23 cm/9 inch circle on a sheet of non-stick baking parchment and place on baking sheets. Cover a third baking sheet with a sheet of non-stick parchment.
2. Whisk the egg whites until very stiff, then gradually whisk in the sugar a spoonful at a time, making sure the meringue is very stiff before adding more sugar.
3. Put the meringue into a piping bag (pastry bag) fitted with a large star vegetable nozzle (tip) and pipe a twisted continuous coil to cover both the parchment circles. Pipe the remaining meringue into 12 whirls on the third

baking sheet. Cook in a cool oven at 110°C/225°F/Gas Mark ¹/₄, allowing 1¹/₂–2 hours for the meringue circles and 1 hour for small meringue whirls. (A fan oven will take about 20 minutes less.) Leave to cool.
4. To make the filling, heat the milk until almost boiling. In a bowl, whisk together the sugar, flour, cornflour

(cornstarch), egg, egg yolk and vanilla flavouring (extract) then whisk in some of the hot milk. Return to the pan and cook very gently, stirring continuously, until very thick. Remove from the heat and stir in the melted chocolate and the rum if using. Cover the mixture with a disc of baking parchment and leave to cool.

5. To assemble the gâteau, place the larger meringue disc on a serving dish and spread evenly with the chocolate custard, then cover with the second meringue disc.
6. Whip the cream until stiff and spread over the the top. Arrange the small meringue whirls around the edge so they just touch each other. Sprinkle the chocolate and nuts (if using) over the centre and decorate with strawberries, if liked. Chill for at least 15 minutes before serving (do not assemble the gâteau more than 1¹/₂ hours before serving).

ZUCCOTTO

A delicious Italian trifle, very rich and very decadent!
It can be prepared in advance and stored in the freezer, but remove at least
1 hour before serving so that it is relatively soft to eat.

INGREDIENTS

Serves 6–8

425 g/14 oz can of stoned (pitted) black cherries, drained, or 500 g/1 lb fresh black cherries, stoned (pitted)
2 tbsp maraschino
2 tbsp water

250 g/8 oz Madeira (pound) cake (see page 95), thinly sliced, or 20 sponge fingers (boudoir biscuits)
3 tbsp orange-flavoured liqueur
600 ml/1 pint/2$^{1}/_{2}$ cups double (heavy) cream
90 g/3 oz/$^{1}/_{2}$ cup caster (superfine) sugar
$^{1}/_{4}$ tsp vanilla flavouring (extract)

45 g/1$^{1}/_{2}$ oz/$^{1}/_{3}$ cup mixed (candied) peel
2 tbsp ground almonds
90 g/3 oz/3 squares dark chocolate, melted and left to cool
2 tbsp rum
60 g/2 oz/$^{1}/_{2}$ cup hazelnuts, chopped

METHOD

1. Put the cherries into a saucepan with the maraschino and water. Bring to the boil, remove from the heat and leave to steep for 10 minutes.

2. Line the sides of a round 1.5 litre/2$^{3}/_{4}$ pint/3 cup bowl

with the cake slices or sponge fingers (boudoir biscuits). Drain the cherries and use the juice to moisten the sponge. Sprinkle the liqueur over the sponge and put in the freezer.

3. Whip one-third of the cream until stiff and stir in half of the sugar, the vanilla flavouring (extract), mixed (candied) peel and ground almonds. Spread in a layer over the sponge base and up the sides. Return to the freezer for 40 minutes until firm.

4. Whip one-third of the cream until just stiff and fold in the cooled melted chocolate, the rum and hazelnuts. Spread this mixture over the cream layer and make a

hole in the centre with a spoon. Return to the freezer.

5. Purée the cherries in a food processor, or mash well by hand, and stir in the rest of the sugar. Whip the remaining cream until stiff and fold in the cherries. Fill the centre of the chocolate and nut mixture with the cream and cherry mixture and return to the freezer for 1 hour, or until ready to

serve. If the zuccotto is kept for longer than 2 hours in the freezer, remove 1 hour before serving. If you do not have a freezer, add a little powdered gelatine to the zuccotto. Dissolve 2 tablespoons or 2 sachets (envelopes) in 120 ml/4 fl oz/$^{1}/_{2}$ cup of hot water in a bowl set over a pan of simmering water. Stir a third of the gelatine into each of the separate mixtures.

6. Unmould on to a chilled dish and serve.

BASIC RECIPES

The same basic recipes may be used in all manner of delicious dishes. The recipes given here are used in many of the desserts in this book, and they can also form the basis for a wide range of other treats.

CHOCOLATE BUTTER CREAM

2 egg yolks
75g/2^1/$_2$ oz/^{1}/$_3$ cup plus 1 tbsp caster (superfine) sugar
4 tbsp water
150 g/5 oz/^{2}/$_3$ cup butter, preferably unsalted and
    slightly softened
90 g/3 oz/3 squares dark chocolate, melted

1. Put the egg yolks into a bowl and beat lightly. Heat the sugar and water in a small saucepan (with a sugar thermometer, if you have one) until the sugar dissolves, then boil rapidly until it reaches 110°C/225°F, or until a small amount placed on a saucer and rolled between finger and thumb forms a strand.
2. As soon as the syrup reaches the correct temperature, pour on to the egg yolks gradually, beating hard all the time. Continue to beat until cold, then add the butter gradually, beating all the time. Finally, add the melted chocolate until smoothly blended. Use at once.

PASTRY CREAM

300 ml/^{1}/$_2$ pint/1^1/$_4$ cups milk
60 g/2 oz/^{1}/$_3$ cup caster (superfine) sugar
1 tbsp plain (all-purpose) flour, sifted
2 tbsp cornflour (cornstarch)
1 egg
1 egg yolk
few drops of vanilla flavouring (extract)
knob of butter

1. Heat the milk gently in a saucepan. Beat the sugar, flour, cornflour (cornstarch), egg and egg yolk together until quite smooth and creamy, then beat in a little of the hot milk. Return the mixture to the saucepan and cook gently, stirring all the time until the mixture thickens and just comes to the boil.
2. Add a few drops of vanilla flavouring (extract) and the butter, and heat gently for 1 minute. Turn the mixture into a bowl. Place a piece of wet baking parchment on the surface to prevent a skin forming.

VARIATIONS

- **For lemon- or orange-flavoured pastry cream,** add the finely grated rind of 2 lemons or 1–2 oranges and a few drops of lemon flavouring (extract) or 1–2 tsp orange flower water.
- **For an almond flavour,** add 45 g/1^1/$_2$ oz/^{1}/$_2$ cup ground almonds and ^{1}/$_2$ teaspoon almond flavouring (extract).

VICTORIA SANDWICH (SPONGE LAYER CAKE)

Makes 18 cm/7 inch cake

125 g/4 oz/^{1}/$_2$ cup butter or margarine
125 g/4 oz/generous ^{1}/$_2$ cup caster (superfine) sugar
2 eggs, beaten
125 g/4 oz/1 cup self-raising flour, sifted
1 tbsp water
few drops of vanilla or other flavouring (extract)
5–6 tbsp raspberry or other jam
icing (confectioners') or caster (superfine) sugar, for
    dredging

1. Lightly grease 2 round sandwich tins (layer pans), 18 cm/7 inches across, and line the bases with non-stick baking parchment.

2. Cream the butter or margarine and sugar together until very light, fluffy and pale.

3. Beat in the eggs, one at a time, following each with a spoonful of the sifted flour.

4. Fold in the remaining flour, followed by the water and vanilla flavouring (extract).

5. Divide the mixture equally between the tins (pans) and level the tops. Bake in a preheated oven at 190°C/375°F/Gas Mark 5 for about 20 minutes, or until well risen, golden brown and firm to the touch. Invert on to a wire rack and leave to cool.

6. When cold, sandwich the 2 cakes together with jam and dredge the top with sifted icing (confectioners') sugar or caster (superfine) sugar. Transfer to a plate to serve.

VARIATIONS

- **Lemon or orange:** Add the grated rind of 1–2 lemons or oranges and replace the water with 1 tablespoon lemon or orange juice.
- **Coffee:** Replace the water with 1 tablespoon coffee flavouring (extract) or very strong black coffee.
- **Chocolate:** Replace 25–30 g/^{3}/$_4$–1 oz/3–4 tablespoons flour with sifted cocoa powder and add ^{1}/$_4$ teaspoon baking powder.

MADEIRA (POUND) CAKE

Makes 18 cm/7 inch round or square cake

175 g/6 oz/^{3}/$_4$ cup butter
175 g/6 oz/^{3}/$_4$ cup caster (superfine) sugar
175 g/6 oz/1^1/$_2$ cups self-raising (self-rising) flour
90 g/3 oz/^{2}/$_3$ cup plain (all-purpose) flour
3 eggs
grated rind of 1–2 lemons
1 tbsp lemon juice
thin slices of candied citron peel (optional)

1. Grease an 18 cm/7 inch round or square deep cake tin (pan) or a 1 kg/2 lb loaf tin (pan) and line the base with non-stick baking parchment.

2. Beat the butter until soft and add the sugar. Cream together until very light and fluffy and pale in colour.

3. Sift the flours together. Beat the eggs into the creamed mixture one at a time, following each with 1 tablespoon of flour.

4. Fold the remaining flour into the cake mixture, followed by the lemon rind and juice. The mixture should be soft but not runny or pourable.

5. Transfer the mixture to the prepared tin (pan), level the top, and add a few slices of citron peel, if using.

6. Bake in a preheated oven at 160°C/325°F/Gas Mark 3 for 1^1/$_2$ hours, or until well risen, firm and browned. Test by inserting a skewer into the cake; it should come out clean if the cake is cooked.

7. Leave the cake to cool in the tin (pan) for about 5 minutes, then invert on to a wire rack and leave until cold. Peel off the paper and store the cake in an airtight container until required.

WHISKED SPONGE CAKE

2-egg mixture:
2 eggs
90 g/3 oz/^{1}/$_2$ cup caster (superfine) sugar
60 g/2 oz/^{1}/$_2$ cup plain (all-purpose) flour

3-egg mixture:
3 eggs
135 g/4^1/$_2$ oz/^{2}/$_3$ cup caster (superfine) sugar
90 g/3 oz/^{2}/$_3$ cup plain (all-purpose) flour

1. Grease, line and flour a baking tin (pan), using the size specified in the recipe.

2. Place the eggs and sugar in a heatproof bowl over a saucepan of boiling water and whisk until the mixture is thick and pale and leaves a trail when the whisk is lifted.

3. Sift and fold in the flour with a metal spoon, then turn the mixture into the tin (pan).

4. Bake in a preheated oven at 190°C/375°F/Gas Mark 5 for 20–25 minutes for the 2-egg mixture and 30 minutes for the 3-egg mixture until the cake springs back when lightly pressed. Turn on to a wire rack to cool.

VARIATIONS

- **For a chocolate whisked sponge cake,** replace 30 g/1 oz/^{1}/$_4$ cup flour with cocoa powder; sift it in with the flour.

INDEX